Lincoln Public Library

December 1979

747

THE WORLDS OF ARCHITECTURAL DIGEST

TRADITIONAL INTERIORS

THE WORLDS OF ARCHITECTURAL DIGEST

TRADITIONAL INTERIORS

EDITED BY PAIGE RENSE

EDITOR-IN-CHIEF, ARCHITECTURAL DIGEST

THE KNAPP PRESS   PUBLISHERS   LOS ANGELES

THE VIKING PRESS   DISTRIBUTORS   NEW YORK

December 1979

Published in the United States of America in 1979
The Knapp Press
5900 Wilshire Boulevard, Los Angeles, California 90036

Distributed by The Viking Press
625 Madison Avenue, New York, New York 10022

Distributed simultaneously in Canada by Penguin Books Canada Limited

Library of Congress Cataloging in Publication Data
Main entry under title: Traditional interiors.
(The Worlds of Architectural digest)
Selections from the pages of Architectural digest, newly edited and designed.
1. Interior decoration. I. Rense, Paige.
II. Architectural digest. III. Series.
NK2130.T7   1979   747'.8'83   79-84682

ISBN 0-89535-034-3
Printed and bound in the United States of America

CONTENTS

FOREWORD

It is hardly a secret that the world in which we live has become increasingly mechanized and given over to technology. In the twentieth century more technological and scientific advances have been made than in all the centuries preceding it, and even the Industrial Revolution pales before the contemporary Age of Computers. Sometimes it seems that everything is new, that none of the old rules applies, that we have completely divorced ourselves from the past. All personal and human factors seem to be taking on less and less importance.

These are some of the reasons why I feel so strongly that traditional décor, in the field of interior design, is of such importance. Indeed, it has been my experience that traditional designs are particularly admired by the readers of ARCHITECTURAL DIGEST. Surely there must be a very good reason for this admiration. Is it because people have little confidence in their own taste? Of course not. Frankly, however, most people feel more comfortable with traditional décor than with the experimentations of contemporary design, as appealing and successful as much of it undeniably is. In a marvelously comforting way, the past is forever there; the rules are established; the mistakes have been eliminated. A sort of purification has taken place, and the trends of the moment have been forgotten. It was inevitable for me to have decided to devote one particular volume in this series to some of the traditional interior design that has appeared, so often and so successfully, in the pages of ARCHITECTURAL DIGEST over the years.

However, it is important for me to make the reasons for this particular selection clear to you. I have been careful to include nothing that is simply a restoration — or an imitation, if you will — of the interior design of the past. To do so would be to offer a book of historical décor when, in fact, another volume in this series is devoted to exactly that proposition. Rather, in consultation with my editors and photographers, with my graphics department and art and antiques experts, I have chosen those designs that reflect all the comfortable certainties of the past while, most importantly, making the past conform to the demands of contemporary life.

It follows that few of the traditional designs in the following pages are "pure" in any academic sense. They are, instead, agreeable adaptations of the past. Many rules have been broken and, paradoxically, many of the results are more contemporary in feeling than anything else. Two examples will, I think, show you what I mean: Pauline de Rothschild's arrangement of her London flat, and the new décor provided by David Hicks for the Irish manor, *Barons Court*. Both these designs simply reflect the past, and they are by no means duplications or imitations. Instead, they are evocations of the past, consciously adjusted to the needs of present-day life. They are intimate, personal and almost defiant in the face of a cold world of technology.

Paige Rense
Editor-in-Chief
Los Angeles, California

THE WORLDS OF ARCHITECTURAL DIGEST

TRADITIONAL INTERIORS

LA MAISON DE SAUSSURE

Great cities, like great families, have a rich private history, and Geneva is no exception to the rule. But, unlike some colorful cities whose past has been obscured by the present, Geneva's history is written large for all to see. In the upper part of the city, known as the Old Town and once the site of a Roman forum, tangible evidence of that history can be found.

Since the Reformation, when Geneva welcomed all those who for reasons of conscience wished to make it their home, the city has had an international character. As time went on, it continued to attract distinguished Europeans, and the eighteenth century brought another great influx, predominantly French. Among the newcomers were some of the most brilliant minds, sharpest wits and most dashing aristocrats in Europe, who in this hospitable atmosphere felt free to sing their songs, expound their theories and write their plays. Along with their intellectual baggage they brought with them their recipes for the good life, the ingredients including beautiful surroundings such as they had enjoyed in France. The big houses of the seventeenth century had been sober and serviceable; the house as display piece had not yet been considered by the Genevans. But now, as this concept came into favor, the city began to plan ensembles of fine townhouses built in the French style. Soon afterward wealthy citizens took up the same idea, constructing great mansions within high walls. When they departed, the owners left these splendid houses as a legacy for future generations, together with the indelible imprint of their culture. And so they remain today.

Perhaps the most magnificent of these houses is *La Maison de Saussure*. Designed by the French architect Abeille for A. J. Lullin, a member of a well-known Geneva family, it took five years to build and was completed in 1712. Later the house passed into the hands of a daughter who was married to Honoré Benedict Saussure, a distinguished Genevan. Today this couple's descendants occupy one entire wing of the house. However, since 1954 Pierre Sciclounoff, a Geneva lawyer and bon vivant who is a friend of the family, has taken over the major part of the mansion. A collector of eighteenth-century art and antique furniture, he has found in these beautifully proportioned rooms an ideal setting for his fine pieces.

The first eleven years of M. Sciclounoff's tenure were given over to restoring the building. The parquet flooring was renewed and the boiseries were restored in the antique way—with wax and overlaid with gold leaf. To make the silk damask that covers the walls and hangs at the French windows of the grand salon, M. Sciclounoff called upon the same weavers who made the silks for Versailles when it was renovated. The crystal chandeliers in all three salons come from the house of the grandfather of Baron de Rothschild. The one in the grand salon has not been electrified, but is lighted by sixty wax candles, which give a soft and flattering glow.

It might well be assumed that La Maison de Saussure has received many guests of historical importance over the years—and it has. One of these was Napoleon, who stopped for three days on his way to the Great St. Bernard Pass. And at one time the tempestuous Madame de Staël lived here with Benjamin Constant, then her lover. During one of their quarrels, Constant attempted to escape her wrath by fleeing down the grand staircase. But the lady ran after him, catching him by the hand when he had almost reached the ground floor. She tugged so hard, and he clung to the balustrade so desperately, that the beautiful iron grillwork was permanently bent. The grillwork is still distorted; the true sense of history has been preserved at La Maison de Saussure.

BELOW: Chinoiserie panels attributed to Pillement and Louis XVI chairs by Pluvinet establish a sense of luxury in the Dining Room. BOTTOM: Walls lined with rare books—most from the 17th and 18th centuries—set off a Louis XVI marquetry bureau à cylindre in the Library.

TOP AND ABOVE: Ornately framed portraits of Rembrandt's father and mother, by followers of the Dutch master, are all from the collection of Pierre Sciclounoff, a Geneva lawyer who has painstakingly restored La Maison de Saussure to its original grandeur.

BELOW: *A light dado heightens the color contrasts that distinguish the sitting area of the Plum Salon. A portrait of Martin Luther by Lucas Cranach suggests piety, while pomp is personified in a representation of the Sun King, Louis XIV, after the Hyacinthe Rigaud original.*

BELOW: *A fire blazes invitingly in the velvet-wrapped Master Bath, appointed with modern tubs encased in polished metal. A Louis XV gilt-bronze cartouche is flanked by figural candelabra on the marble mantel; biscuit de Saint-Cloud sculptures maintain a formal symmetry.*

LEFT: *In a Sitting Room of the master suite, walls covered in menswear serge establish a muted background for a collection of paintings grouped around two Houdon stone sculptures, each accompanied by its clay maquette. Suede-upholstered furniture is clustered in the center of the room among clear glass tables laden with small boxes and rare objects. An Aubusson rug and a Louis XV footstool contribute warm color accents.*

SAN FRANCISCO STYLE

On a corner lot across from the lovely greenery of Alta Plaza Park in the Pacific Heights section of San Francisco stands a brown shingle Victorian house designed by architect Willis Polk in 1897 and formerly lived in by interior designer Val Arnold. There are other Polk houses on the narrow streets of San Francisco, but this one — built as a country home in the heart of the city—is the one Mr. Arnold coveted. "Years ago I saw the doors open, walked in and said, 'Someday I am going to live here.'"

The three-story house is a historical landmark, having served as a hospital during the great earthquake of 1906. It forms an elongated H, with a central hall and staircase dividing nineteen rooms — an arrangement that afforded a "separate but equal" quality to the designer's living and working areas. From every window there is a vista of green grass and trees, and the view of the park across the street is an integral part of the whole.

The living room itself was a result of his preference for a nighttime ambience. Originally a dining room, it was converted by lacquering and glazing the walls. "It was difficult to do," says the designer, "because the wood was redwood, but even though it didn't match the molding, it blended well. When you looked into the room, your first impression was that it was paneled." It is the largest room in the house, measuring seventeen by twenty-seven feet — sizable by nineteenth-century standards, but not by contemporary ones. However, Mr. Arnold's décor for it was a perfect expression of his convictions about scale: "If you have a small room, plan it within an inch of its life and treat it like a large room," he says. "On the other hand, if you have a spacious room, use less but larger furniture. There is, for example, a studio apartment in New York, done by Billy Baldwin, that is the most beautiful room I have ever seen. It is a brown-and-black room, no more than twelve by twenty feet, but he's filled it up with big pieces of furniture and used every inch of wall space. So you see how very important scale is in really fine design and decoration."

The most difficult decisions in Val Arnold's own house centered around the bedroom. "Doing that room was a major project. It was agony, and I tried everything. First I put in a lot of heavy molding. Then I tried about fifty different fabrics. Then I consulted designer friends like Tony Hail and Michael Taylor. At last I ran across a plaid fabric, and everything came together. But I kept wondering why I had been unable to reach a decision."

Then he realized that he, like many of his clients, had been a victim of his past. When he was twelve years old, he was allowed to decorate his own room. At that time he chose plaid spreads not unlike the plaid fabric he used in his Pacific Heights bedroom. At twelve he painted his walls forest green; the later bedroom's walls were a deep green-black. "But," says the designer, "I certainly wasn't aware of the parallels when I was doing that room." An understanding of his own reactions has given him a greater insight into client indecision. He knows that there are many ways to resolve design dilemmas, but feels the reasons for their existence are seldom obvious. "Based on my own experience, the solution became more obvious. I discovered, with many clients, that if I can pull them back to a room where they have been happy, a decision can be reached."

Looking into the future of interior design, Val Arnold feels that everyone is becoming slightly bored with glass and plastic, and little can be accomplished with waves of nostalgia. "I've seen people with everything in the world, and it has made them no happier. Personally, I try for simplicity."

This Victorian house in San Francisco's Pacific Heights, formerly owned by designer Val Arnold, served as a refugee hospital after the earthquake of 1906. PRECEDING PAGE: *Mr. Arnold set the Living Room's colors aglow with a carefully designed system of spotlighting.*

BELOW: *Mr. Arnold's collection of pre-Columbian art recalled the past, while the designer's hothouse plants and blooms added a touch of vitality. A greenhouse was built on the deck outside the bedroom to supply the thriving plants displayed throughout the house.*

OPPOSITE: *Once the 19-room residence's dining room, the Living Room became an ideal environment for relaxing or socializing. Walls lacquered and glazed to simulate wood paneling, richly patterned carpet, verdant plants and a shimmering brass Flemish chandelier all contributed to the room's subtle blend of colors and textures.*

BELOW: *The Dining Room illustrated the designer's theory on the handling of a small room: "Treat it like a big room." Here, the fearless use of bold pattern and color in the paisley wallcovering was softened by the glow of candlelight. The narrow table and tall chairs fit the space perfectly.*

OPPOSITE: *The rich yet understated atmosphere of the Library exemplified Mr. Arnold's preference for a harmonious mixture of medium tones and values. Simple bowls and terra-cotta objects were placed on a French-style desk flanked by a pair of Régence cane-back chairs.*

BELOW: *Lively detailing created refreshing foils for the Bedroom's dark walls. Light-painted molding and mantel stood out vividly; checkered fabric covered the bed and sofa, and Imari porcelains graced an 18th-century mule chest and a 16th-century Italian bench.*

OPPOSITE: *An alcove in the bedroom provided a cheerful, secluded work space with windows opening onto a peaceful view of the foliage outside the house and of the park across the street. Light-colored shutters and more of the same checkered drapery fabric used throughout the room brightened the area.* RIGHT: *A pleasing assemblage of marble spheres made an artistic tabletop arrangement.*

SUTTON PLACE TOWNHOUSE

Nestled in privacy on the bank of the East River in Manhattan, Sutton Place has managed to retain an atmosphere of quiet isolation rich with the echoes of another time and place. It seems strangely, and fortunately, removed from the skyscrapers and the concrete and the tempo of New York. Paradoxically, of all the attractive residential areas in the city, Sutton Place is at once the most typical of old New York and the most international in character. Though the locale is American, a few changes of background could easily transform it into Chelsea along the Thames or the Ile de la Cité in the Seine.

So it is by no means eccentric or inappropriate that the owners of a four-story Georgian Colonial townhouse on Sutton Place chose the advice of Italian interior designer Lorenzo Mongiardino. Although his main offices are in Milan, he is definitely an international designer; his projects range regularly from his own country to England and Switzerland, to France and to the United States.

As is typical of European interior designers, his early career ranged farther afield than those of his counterparts in the United States. Born in Genoa, he began school there at the Politecnico and went on to Milan to study architecture. At the beginning of his career he concentrated on designing sets for theater and films rather than on the interior décor that is his métier today. His work in films was notable for some stunning successes, especially the sets he designed for Franco Zeffirelli in the Italian films of Shakespeare's *The Taming of the Shrew* and *Romeo and Juliet*. With such a varied background in the field of design, Lorenzo Mongiardino has been able to bring to interior décor a depth of experience and expertise, an extensive knowledge of architecture and a theatrical flair that the average decorator does not often have at his command.

This background served him particularly well when he came to consider the Sutton Place project. In some ways it was a lovely stage set, already partially completed: a handsome townhouse almost entirely surrounded by trees, with a garden running down to the edge of the river. And the "props" he was given to work with included a collection of art that would distinguish any house in any part of the world: paintings by Utrillo, Rouault, Modigliani, Matisse, Dufy, Kandinsky, Bacon — the list is seemingly endless. In addition, the period furniture and accessories arranged by Sr. Mongiardino and his associate Fiorenzo Cattaneo encompass a wide range of periods and styles: Queen Anne mirrors, Regency lanterns, Degas bronzes, Louis XVI clocks, nineteenth-century Bessarabian rugs, rare East India Company fabrics, English Victoriana.

"I am *not* a decorator," says Lorenzo Mongiardino emphatically. "I have no specific, no unmistakable style. As a matter of fact, I would hate to have anyone walk into a house I have done and say, 'This is a Mongiardino.' Don't misunderstand," he adds. "I have the highest respect for the great decorators. It just isn't what I do. For example, take the house on Sutton Place. For many years now I have been working on old houses with a great deal of pleasure. Really, they have become my main interest, and practically all my work lies in the area of restoration. I want to turn these wonderful old houses into places where people can live today."

Set designer, student of old houses, magician, Lorenzo Mongiardino has produced on Sutton Place an ambience entirely appropriate to locale. He has overseen a mixture of many styles and periods with the skill of his long familiarity in many areas of design, and he has conjured up no less than a home of exceeding comfort, charm and permanence.

24

A timeless grace pervades Lorenzo Mongiardino's design of a four-story townhouse on Manhattan's Sutton Place. OPENING PAGE AND LEFT: *In the Living Room, a blend of patterns creates a lively background for artworks by such modern masters as Renoir, Degas and Monet.*

27

PRECEDING PAGES: *Cheerful floral upholstery fabric and draperies and a warm-hued Aubusson rug are bright foils for the 18th-century English pine paneling in the Dining Room/Library. Daylight streams through a trio of French doors that reveal a view of the parklike garden.*

ABOVE AND RIGHT: *Gilded fretwork panels interspersed with painted-on silver-leaf flowers add brilliance to the fourth-floor Sitting Room. Caspar Netscher's portrait entitled* A Princess of Orange—*mounted on a mirror above a Louis XV bombé commode—is artfully reflected in another mirror surrounding the églomisé-paneled mantelpiece at the opposite end of the room.*

OPPOSITE AND BELOW: *Modigliani's portrait of Lunia Czechowska graces one wall of the Study, which also houses a Rouault clown, a Bacon head and a Utrillo cityscape.* BOTTOM: *The Parlor provides a cheerful setting for works by Matisse, Dufy and Signac.*

In the Master Bedroom, an unusual mix of heterogeneous patterns contributes a sense of long-established comfort. The pièce de résistance, a Hepplewhite four-poster bed, extends this mood: Its canopy frame is painted with Neo-Classical motifs, while its 19th-century English patchwork quilt combines geometric shapes with flowers.

DICKENSIAN CHARM IN LONDON

"If you have enough to buy a loaf of bread, buy half a loaf and spend the rest on lilies," says antiques dealer Stephen Long cheerfully. It is a maxim he heard a persuasive saleswoman quote to a customer in a Chinese art shop where he was once employed. When he left the shop, he opened a stall in London's Portobello Market, and then, some fifteen years ago, launched his own antiques business in Chelsea. When he started, the area known as Little Chelsea was unfashionable. Today it is a mecca for treasure hunters, and his little shop on the ground floor of his early-Victorian house is most successful.

After coming down from Oxford, Mr. Long began his career as a schoolmaster, but he is most content living as he does today. He enjoys dealing in objects, sometimes bringing them into his home to stay a while, perhaps keeping some, and placing others in the shop below to pass into other hands. In his living quarters his skill as a perceptive buyer is there for all to see. Although furniture, books and ornaments attract the eye from every corner, they do not jostle irritably for position because the owner has carefully placed them in happy order. In the softly lit living room there is something of the atmosphere of the schoolmaster's study. Here, on a night when the wind is rattling the roof slates, the room with its fireplace is snug and inviting. One hears a taxi outside as it passes through the wet streets—a sound especially evocative of foggy London town.

Above all, luxury is what Stephen Long wants in a room. He admits that living alone makes him selfish. "I am very self-indulgent," he says. "I love masses of flowers and plants everywhere—a room is like a good garden in this respect. And I like matches galore, and ashtrays, a well-stocked bar and lots of ice. I love bath essences, sachets and lavender bags amongst the linen, delicious smells like Rigaud candles and Mary Chess perfume. I like to be cool, but when it's really cold outside I love to have a roaring log fire. And I always use pink-tinted electric light bulbs to add a warm feeling.

"I prefer formal arrangements—bold lines and groupings, softened by lots of clutter," the designer continues. "I hate shapeless chairs, furniture quaintly askew and any sort of fancy lampshade. I do not personally like grand or glittering objects. Of course, this may be rationalization, but I'd rather have something a bit battered, as long as it appeals." He does not want priceless possessions and is not bothered by the odd hairline crack. Life is short, he seems to be saying, so enjoy it and eat from the bowl while it's in one piece. "I'm hopelessly extravagant," says Mr. Long. "I believe in being as comfortable as possible and enjoying myself. But I do have to curtail the spending once in a while!"

He did all the decorating of the Chelsea house himself, wielding the brush while listening to Mozart on the record player. It is his private joke that designer friends think he used expert painters.

When asked about influences on his concept of décor, Mr. Long first mentions the renowned interior designer, the late John Fowler. Of Fowler's work he says, "It is English decoration at its very best." Mario Praz, the Italian writer, is another influence, and although his books are alleged to cast an evil eye on their surroundings, Stephen Long is not concerned with such notions. He also enjoys reading about the 1930s, and is fascinated by the work of Syrie Maugham and Elsie de Wolfe.

When discussing what style and taste are, Stephen Long makes it clear that he has achieved his own exact and personal blend in a cozy setting. "Good taste is what *you* enjoy," he says emphatically. "It is simply a question of finding your own niche."

A medley of favorite objects brightens antiques dealer Stephen Long's Victorian home in London's Little Chelsea.
PRECEDING PAGE: *Bookshelves crowned by busts of such worthies as Shakespeare and Milton set off a dense tabletop pastiche in the Sitting Room.*

RIGHT: *A sunny-hued background and* faux *tortoiseshell moldings warm the sitting room, where pieces from Mr. Long's extensive porcelain collection are displayed on every surface. The mid-19th-century Wilton rug, emblazoned with royal emblems, once adorned a floor in Buckingham Palace.*

Another view of the Sitting Room is highlighted by a somber triple portrait of Charles I, after Van Dyke. Books, paintings and an accumulation of Old World objects illustrate the owner's penchant for "formal arrangements softened by lots of clutter."

LEFT: Faux marbre *vitrines displaying a collection of Leeds and Wedgwood creamware flank a mirrored wall, its center occupied by a Regency convex mirror that reflects the Dining Room in miniature.* OPPOSITE: *In the Master Bedroom, still more gilt-framed paintings and drawings, well-laden bookshelves and a variety of porcelain objects reflect Mr. Long's diverse enthusiasms. A cheerful chintz fabric drapes the head of the bed.*

AMALGAM OF OLD AND NEW

As a young man in Spain, Paco Muñoz Cabrero studied architecture and stage design. But nothing seemed to attract him to the career of interior design until, with his friend the Vizconde de Fefiñanes, he founded a company called Casa y Jardin, devoted to interior design and the manufacture of furniture. The company was an enormous success.

Today Sr. Muñoz has a number of houses himself, in addition to his residence in Madrid: one in the small town of Pedraza, a walled medieval castle that formerly belonged to the painter Zuloaga; another in Majorca, on the Costa de los Piños overlooking the sea; and still another in Marbella, on the Mediterranean coast. None of the houses is at all similar to the others; each has a particular feeling and style appropriate to its locale. Such variety is a happy indication that the designer is a man without preconceived opinions who has the facility of adapting his talents to a special set of circumstances.

The house in Madrid is a good example. It is located on a quiet street in one of the central areas of the capital. Built in the middle years of the nineteenth century, it contains only two stories and was designed to be occupied by one family. The foyer gives an immediate and exact picture of the approach to décor favored by Paco Muñoz. Above all, it is notable for its sense of proportion and its sobriety. A large English table occupies most of one wall, and on its top is a display of obelisks. In the center of the hall there is a zebra platform, a place to sit for a moment or leave an overcoat. The furnishings and objects here are of the finest quality, as they are in all the rooms throughout the house.

When asked which of his many roles he prefers — company director, businessman, industrialist, decorator — Sr. Muñoz says without hesitation that he prefers interior design. "Apart from Casa y Jardin,

which today is a complex of various companies with more than four hundred employees, I own three public relations firms. And I naturally design furniture and fabrics and accessories for Casa y Jardin. All of these things," he explains, "are of course intimately connected with interior design. But really it is décor itself that interests me the most. It is essential to understand how to use volume, how to manipulate the space at your disposal. A certain rhythm is necessary, a sense of balance, an understanding of color. I think a designer should know as much as possible about everything that has been made in the world, and about everything that is being made today. Not that there is any question of copying someone else's work, but a certain familiarity with all aspects of design and its history is basic. This knowledge gives the designer a confidence that allows him to achieve a result so harmonious that it seems spontaneous and natural.

"And also I think it important for an interior designer to have studied architecture to some extent and to be familiar with its general techniques," Sr. Muñoz continues. "I do feel that without such training one runs the risk of producing amateur results. You see, in a way, a decorator is a sort of doctor for architecture. When the architecture is good, I try to emphasize and respect it without distractions. Bad architecture, on the other hand, will require a certain amount of camouflage."

Certainly Paco Muñoz follows his own principles to the letter, and his house in Madrid serves as an excellent illustration. There is an air of harmony and tranquillity about it, along with a strong contemporary feeling that nonetheless respects all the lovely antique elements of the house itself. The result may seem effortless, but a lifetime of study and experimentation stands behind it.

In the mid-19th-century Madrid home of interior designer Paco Muñoz, elements of the past are blended strikingly with contemporary influences. PRECEDING PAGE: *A handpainted ceiling medallion and lacquered treillage ornament the Victorian-style Central Hall.*

ABOVE: *In the brilliantly painted Foyer, a mixture of Syrian obelisks atop a Regency library table, Japanese stack tables and a painted wood construction by José Ignacio Cardenas makes an exuberant welcoming statement.* OPPOSITE: *Unobtrusive spotlights placed ingeniously in the original ornate ceiling of the central hall highlight both modern and antique appointments.*

Paco Muñoz's ability to mix eras is especially evident in this view of the Central Hall, where gracefully tall windows provide a backdrop for a glass and steel bar and a handsome English reading stand. Indoor palms in cube planters shelter an antique British Colonial daybed.

A large collection of gleaming antique scientific and measuring instruments is displayed in one of four identical steel, brass and glass étagères in the Living Room. An Egyptian head on the bottom shelf stands out in stark contrast to the dramatically dark handmade wallcovering.

47

The Living Room's deep tones provide a neutral background for a bold use of geometric patterns. A Sheraton globe stands near an 18th-century English architect's table that holds small sculptures; the engraving hanging above it is by Chillida.

WARM PALETTE FOR OREGON

The sun casts a mist-shrouded light over the city and the fog swirls everywhere, blurring houses, turning sidewalks the color of pewter, impelling the trees, forever green, to a height and breadth more often found in forests than in cities. Pedestrians are bent against the chilling dampness. Portland, Oregon, is not a city for casual strolling. Nor is it one of long standing, like New York or Washington. Perhaps because of its rugged history, Portland exhibits considerably more vitality than many older, more genteel cities; while easterners were starching antimacassars, Oregonians were blazing trails. Today Portland is a city still surrounded by natural beauty, and one where cloudy days are a way of life.

Anyone in need of interior designers who can make the most of this particular location and climate could do no better than to turn to skilled colorists Kalef Alaton and Janet Polizzi, whose offices are in Los Angeles. "In Oregon you have whole weeks and months without sunshine," says Mr. Alaton. "It was essential to think about ways to offset and compensate for the cold weather." The house he and his partner decorated in Portland was purchased for its dramatic view. It is high on a hill, with a feeling of complete isolation; the city lies below, and the sky is suspended at eye level. Understanding the potential, the designers created walls of an indeterminate, pale, but definitely warm color. "Except for the master bedroom," says Kalef Alaton, "the color exists only on the walls. We did not repeat it in the fabric, furniture or rugs." The color works its magic by intensifying light; a slight blue cast to the sky can fill the rooms with an illusion of sunshine, almost making it seem as if the house were in a warm climate. In addition, the ceiling of the garden room is mirrored—not for the usual reason of increasing the feeling of space, but to capture the light. It is a room that creates an image of the outdoors, and the only one in the house with plants. "When you have a good house," explains Kalef Alaton, "you like to have an atmosphere of plants and flowers, but they are not really a necessity."

The designers completed each room with a careful selection of objects, chosen to create light where there was none before. It is a house they describe as being filled with *grand cachet,* to which the quality of woods, crystal, silver and fabric all contribute. "It is a secret of design that you discover slowly," says Mr. Alaton. "To my mind the house has an abundant, and very human, quality. This takes many forms. For example, when you walk into a room, I think you have the feeling you have been here before. That is a far different feeling from walking into a room and being stunned by it. No matter how beautifully designed such a room may be, there is little emotion about it—you don't feel a part of it.

"In this house, however," Mr. Alaton continues, "I think that things are very different. For example, when the house was finished the owners gave a party, and one guest said, 'This is your house. How could it have been any other way?' That is a great compliment for us as interior designers. To know that a house is right, that the design has solved the problems and that there is no question or doubt about it gives me pleasure. You see, I'm not interested in simply doing one more project. I enjoy my work because of the feelings I get from it. What I do always seems to become part of myself."

And it is with this perception that Kalef Alaton and Janet Polizzi strive to design environments expressly intended for human comfort and enjoyment. In the case of this Portland house, they have succeeded admirably: They have created a sunlit world far removed from the gray climate outdoors.

In this hilltop home high above Portland, Oregon, designers Kalef Alaton and Janet Polizzi compensated for the cold, gray Northwest climate by capturing a sense of warmth in the décor. PRECEDING PAGE: A mirrored ceiling maximizes the light in the Garden Room.

BELOW: The floral patterns of the draperies, upholstery and antique Persian carpet animate the Living Room, while pale earth-toned walls heighten the natural lighting. The warmth of velvet, silk and chintz is counterbalanced by the cool black granite of the table.

BELOW: *When weather permits, the iron-railed Terrace is a vantage point at mealtime. With nothing more than a sculptured maiden to intrude, a leisurely breakfast under the outstretched branches of a shade tree offers both privacy and a panoramic vista of the city below.*

53

BELOW: *Mirrors extend the space in the Master Bath. The reflection in the far wall reveals an antique Venetian mirror hanging above a dressing table, and an airily draped window admits a view of cascading greenery — one of the bonuses of Oregon's rainy weather.*

RIGHT: *In the Master Bedroom, elaborate antique columns — redesigned to serve as posts for the canopied bed — accentuate the vertical thrust created by the neutral draperies. The subtle color scheme of the quilted fabrics, upholstery and appointments characterizes the tone set throughout the entire residence. The 17th-century portrait is the work of a Russian court artist.*

BARONS COURT

When he wanted to alter *Barons Court,* the family home in Ireland, the marquess of Hamilton consulted interior designer David Hicks, a master of the modern stately home. "David walked in, asked for a glass of port and the plans of the house—and, after only a brief tour, made all the right decisions in half an hour," says Lord Hamilton. That, of course, is something of an exaggeration, as it takes considerably more than half an hour even to walk around Barons Court. What is true is that Mr. Hicks immediately saw through the formality of the plans to a sensible scheme that would make the house work beautifully in the twentieth century.

The duke and duchess of Abercorn, two very modern people, had decided that the time was right to share the house with their son James, marquess of Hamilton, his wife and their two children. The duke and duchess have kept their favorite rooms on one side of the house, and it is on the other side that the greatest changes have taken place.

Indeed, change is one of the traditions of Barons Court. The present restorations are the most recent in a series of changes made to the house over the years, and many hands have contributed. The house was built for the Abercorn family in 1730 and then remodeled by Sir John Soane, architect of the Bank of England, in 1791. Over the years the damage from two great fires necessitated extensive renovations, but the basic structure has remained the same.

Today each of the rooms has its own strength and character, imposed by the architecture itself but carefully reinforced by the colors Lady Hamilton and David Hicks have chosen. The designer explains: "I suggested; she decided." Thus the library has become a place in which to linger, to sit in a well-used leather chair and read or have coffee after dinner. The colors of the leather-bound books—

thousands of them, all catalogued by Christie's—encourage a mood of quietness. On the walls is old velvet, soft with the sheen of the years when it saw service as curtains in the former state dining room, and on the floor is a geometric carpet designed by Mr. Hicks. In contrast, the Long Gallery, which opens off the library, offers a most lovely invitation to walk, to admire. Its ninety-two-foot length presents a dazzling space filled with creamy colors, paced off by ten windows, two sets of Corinthian columns and a progression of pastels for the different groups of furniture. Upstairs the colors are also soft, and corridors stretch out like flower beds.

After two years of work, the rooms were restored. Then, for the entire family, began the pleasures of putting things back into place. Strong, good-natured workers carried heavy loads of marble and furniture about the house while everyone gave cheerfully conflicting advice. David Hicks, with his fine eye for arrangement, acted as traffic director and Lady Hamilton, making regular trips to the greenhouse across the parkland, had the enviable task of choosing the household greenery from among hundreds of geraniums, jasmine, rare clematis.

Barons Court has always been a happy house, not even able to claim a ghost—except for an ethereal spaniel rumored to frisk about in the upper reaches. Family memories are of Christmas trees in the entrance hall and sleigh rides with bells jingling. This genial life continues there today. An elegant victoria has been restored for pony rides around the three lakes, and on warm summer afternoons there is swimming, water skiing or a row upon the lakes with baskets of sandwiches and cakes carefully stowed away for tea. Children are still dancing to the player piano, and the joyous spirit of Barons Court lives now as it did long ago.

Barons Court, the Abercorn family estate in Ireland, dates from 1730. Designer David Hicks revitalized the stately residence for 20th-century living while still preserving the heritage of the past. PRECEDING PAGE: *The Entrance Hall's Neo-Classic ceiling was created by Sir Richard Morrison in the 1840s. The 18th-century rocking horse's strange rattle has mystified generations of children.* BELOW: *The 1791 Long Gallery is punctuated by ornate Corinthian columns. Mr. Hicks restored the room to its original grandeur by opening formerly partitioned areas.*

A fireplace wall in the Long Gallery displays an eclectic blend of ornaments, including a Louis XV-style mantel and a 1790s parcel-gilt mirror. Elegant 18th-century trompe l'oeil cutout wooden figures serve as fire screens. Sèvres cachepots hold estate-grown rhododendrons.

In the Staircase Hall, vividly lacquered walls highlight the imposingly scaled suspended staircase designed by Morrison. On the left wall is a hunting scene by Sir Edward Landseer; above are family portraits. Under the staircase is a gilded 15th-century Italian cassone.

*A Hicks-designed round rug and the domed ceiling
designed by Morrison emphasize the shape of the Rotunda
Dining Room. Encircled by Ionic columns, the room is
now the setting for dinner parties and family celebrations.
The chairs were made for the first duke of Abercorn.*

In the Master Bedroom, the glazed chintz fabric used for drapes and cornices is a Hicks reproduction of an 1850s design. Carefully balanced 18th-century mezzotints hang above the Regency mahogany tables flanking the window, which frames a view of the gentle Irish landscape.

The bright spaciousness of a Guest Room is emphasized by its "tray" ceiling, designed by Sir John Soane in 1791. Victorian brass bedsteads are draped with delicately printed cotton, sweeping softly toward a fine vista of terraced gardens. The carpeting is Irish Tretford cord.

A COUNTRY VILLA IN PERIGORD

In the southwest of France was the ancient feudal domain of Périgord, roughly equivalent to the present Dordogne. Perhaps it is the one part of France where a feeling of the past is most clearly preserved, for little seems to have changed over the centuries. Small fortified towns still guard the riverbanks, lost hamlets slumber in the forest and tiny villages are grouped around Norman churches.

However, in the last twenty years many new people have discovered the delights of Périgord. It has attracted English, Dutch, French from the north and, lately, a few Americans. Some have bought châteaux overlooking the Dordogne, others farmhouses in forest clearings. Some have even bought entire abandoned villages, thus providing individual houses for guests and children. Nevertheless, this does not mean that Périgord has suddenly become the fashionable place to go. Residents are extremely jealous of their isolation.

Certainly this is one of the reasons why Serge Royaux, one of the busiest interior designers in Paris, chooses to have a country house in this remote and unspoiled province of France. The characteristics of Périgord—simplicity, the use of sturdy materials and sober colors—quite naturally attract a designer whose own work has always been severe and understated. Indeed, his style is reminiscent of the fashion designs of one of his first clients, the couturier Balenciaga. It is easy to recognize a Royaux interior, whether in the Schlumberger bank, the French Embassy in Washington or the Robert Lehman wing of the Metropolitan Museum of Art. A certain simplicity is all-pervasive, in essence more luxurious than all the elaborate ornamentation put together by decorators who merely copy the past.

M. Royaux never tries to re-create a Louis XVI salon or an Empire bedroom. Rather, he uses Louis XVI or Empire furniture only when it is appropriate to a given interior, be it an apartment in Paris or a villa in Provence. He is fond of covering large sofas with the same material used for draperies, providing counterpoints with black window latches and door handles and bright cushions. His interiors are often done in white or in one of the shades favored by Balenciaga: dark brown, garnet red or velvet black. Above all, the designer uses elements that bring to mind the architect more than the upholsterer.

Each of these hallmarks can be seen in *La Sudrie*, the house in the heart of Périgord that Serge Royaux and his wife, Anne, bought some years ago. Dating from 1710, the beautiful Louis XIV house has been restored with the elegant simplicity it merits, and no attempt has been made to give it an artificial "country" look. Only the large kitchen with its stone floor and huge fireplace is authentically rustic. Copper pots hang from the walls, hams are suspended from the great beams and stone crocks filled with pâté and preserved meats are lined up on the shelves.

The house itself is very simple. A large ground floor with tall, small-paned windows opens onto a terrace overlooking the woods and surrounding countryside. A hallway divides the house in two. On one side are the living room, the dining room and the kitchen; on the other, the library and the bedrooms. The library is filled with books by all those marvelous authors read in childhood—Jules Verne, Alexandre Dumas, Sir Walter Scott.

In some ways, perhaps, a visit to Périgord is like a return to a beautiful time, complete with those wonderful old houses where the armoires were always full of candy jars and children played hide-and-seek in the hallways. Here, M. Royaux has created a home that incorporates the comforts of a country retreat with the sophistication of fine design.

LEFT: *A spare simplicity governs the Entrance Hall, which is enlivened by a gaggle of wooden waterfowl, wide-brimmed straw hats and a cluster of canes and walking sticks. Painted 17th-century boiserie, waxed brick flooring and a brass chandelier quietly emphasize the house's historical authenticity.*

LEFT: *Framed by the geometric boiserie, an 18th-century poultry-shop sign functions as a pure-spirited artwork in the entrance hall. Together with the collection of duck decoys, it introduces a unifying motif that appears in related guises throughout the residence.*

Flanking the Living Room fireplace, a pair of fabric-covered, nail-ornamented folding screens extends the geometry of the boiserie and restates the neutral tones of the Louis XIII sofa and chairs. Dark wood accents anchor lighter elements and add a muted rusticity.

RIGHT: *A Living Room ensemble is a testamonial to fine craftsmanship. The table displays 18th- and 19th-century turned-wood objects; the Henry II chest, behind, reflects a masterly carving tradition.*

BELOW: *Like all the antiques in the residence, the Library's Louis XIV boiserie is indigenous to the environs, having come from a neighboring château. Louis XIII and Louis XIV appointments reaffirm the historical atmosphere, yet their simplified lines are paradoxically modern in character.*

ABOVE: *In the Dining Room, a stark Caen stone chimneypiece and a blazing fire create an archetypal country background for repasts enjoyed at a large Louis XIII convent table. Antique faïence from Choisy—the floral centerpiece, garniture and flowerlike plates—mingle with 18th-century Venetian glassware in a bright, informal table setting.* ABOVE RIGHT: *A balanced composition of 19th-century farm implements of the region adds rugged beauty to an entrance wall.* BELOW RIGHT: *Dark latches provide a decorative counterpoint to pristine cupboards in the large Kitchen. Suspended above the antique country table and chairs is a collection of locally made baskets.*

OPPOSITE LEFT: *Dark-light contrasts animate a Guest Room appointed with Louis XIII armchairs, a canopy bed and, on the mantel, a pair of generous faïence jars.*
OPPOSITE RIGHT: *The Bath combines modern and antique features. Shutters and checkered wallcovering, baskets overhead and grasses under glass reinforce the flavor of the age-worn glazed bricks surrounding the tub and washbasin. The Louis XIII table and chair are both decorative and functional.*

OPPOSITE AND RIGHT: *Copied from an 18th-century prototype, the floral fabric used throughout Mme. Royaux's Bedroom establishes a warm, patterned background for sturdy wooden surfaces. Ornamental highlights include a small family of duck decoys, a 15th-century pietà, the English chandelier, and bed finials that reach to the ceiling.*

A PRINCESS AT HOME IN PARIS

Princess Ghislaine de Polignac and the Baron de Cabrol, her interior designer and a friend of long standing, are both well-known members of *Tout-Paris*, that glamorous inner circle of Parisian society in which the first considerations are those of style and taste. Even more importantly, however, both are renowned for their kindness and their charm, qualities more and more difficult to find in today's hurried world. Although they share an enthusiasm for the elegant life, they abhor pretension of any kind. There is no doubt that their tastes are extravagant, but they instinctively understand how to create the most luxurious of atmospheres casually and without ostentation. Everything seems effortlessly arranged, so that new friends feel every bit as welcome and at ease as old ones.

Perhaps because there is something a trifle theatrical in the fabric of her glamorous life, the princess has chosen to decorate her salon in a manner at once sumptuous and intimate, which suggests nothing so much as a box at the theater. The room is entirely done in red, for the artist Christian Bérard once told her that she "must always be careful to mix many different shades of red," and she has followed his advice to the letter. The great sofa with its large pillows suggests the last row of seats in an opera box, and the generous use of mirrors also enhances the room's theatricality. The ingenuity of the interior designer must be admired. He has created any number of false perspectives, thus succeeding in making the apartment seem far larger than it really is: An infinity of excitement is suggested. Through the use of mirrors even the entrance hall becomes a picture gallery, with its reflections of the paintings in the salon and of the princess's many elegant guests. The mirrors reflect other delights as well: small gilt chairs, highly polished mahogany chests, green plants in bright silver cachepots. This profusion of subtly gleaming appointments immediately recalls the opulent décor of Napoleon III's Second Empire.

It is in this style—considerably simplified, to be sure—that Fred de Cabrol has decorated the princess's salon, duplicating that mélange of other periods and other styles so characteristic of the Second Empire. But one of M. de Cabrol's great talents as an interior designer is his ability to recreate the décor of another era without overdoing it. He is able to adapt the past to the contemporary scene, keeping all the elements of vanished grandeur yet never indulging in a purely period décor. Actually, only serious collectors will have rooms that are impeccable Louis XV or Empire. The Baron de Cabrol, on the other hand, knows how to mix styles with charm and elegance, and it is such a mixture that he has provided for the Princess de Polignac.

Since the baron and his wife are enthusiastic about hunting and riding, he often incorporates sporting prints into his interior designs. This penchant, along with a lavish use of chintz, creates the atmosphere of an English country house. It is a mood that can also be found in the Princess de Polignac's bedroom, since her family, too, is devoted to horses and riding. But in spite of a generous use of polished wood in the English manner, and of many sporting prints, the bedroom is definitely that of a beautiful woman, feminine in every way. Slipped into the fabric-covered frame of her bedroom mirror are some of the many invitations she constantly receives to dinners and gallery openings. There is about the bedroom, as about the whole apartment, an air of elegant festivity. And, indeed, Ghislaine de Polignac always has a bottle of champagne, properly chilled and nestled in a large silver bucket, ready for any of her friends to join her for an evening of merriment.

OPPOSITE: *An 18th-century lacquer bureau plat in the Salon holds souvenirs of the princess's active life. Paintings by the 18th-century artists Nattier and Largillière are prominently displayed.* BELOW: *A lavish Louis XVI clock and ormolu candelabra ornament the mantel.*

LEFT: *A grouping of 18th- and 19th-century French and English paintings hangs above a bookcase lined with tooled leather volumes.* ABOVE: *Bright upholstery and carpeting with a paisley motif are a vivid background for an eclectic mix of styles in the salon. Among the works of art that grace the room is a portrait by Clairin of the princess's grandfather in military dress.*

In the Dining Room, the richness of deep-hued walls
and a lacquer console is amplified by shimmering Louis
XVI crystal girandoles. An elegant 18th-century French
portrait smiles across the room, while velvet-upholstered
chairs and tall Chinese vases provide cool contrast.

77

FAR LEFT AND BOTTOM: *A mellow warmth envelops the Bedroom, with its patterned sofa and draperies, invitation-decked mirror, and family photographs and memorabilia. A soft pastel portrait of the princess's brother hangs on the mirror.* LEFT AND BELOW: *Seating plans designed for splendid occasions line a silk-covered wall. A detail shows one of the princess's fancifully calligraphic guest lists.*

IN THE ALLEGHENY FOOTHILLS

Located in the rustic Allegheny Mountain foothills east of Pittsburgh, *Woodlea* is a hundred-acre estate surrounded by state game lands and extensive private property. The courtly hilltop residence commands sweeping vistas of manicured fields and thick woods, where the stillness is broken only by songbirds and the gentle splashing of water into a pool. In the early evening deer feed close to the house, and wild turkeys wander by.

Interior designer Gertrude A. Mellon adapted the Colonial-style residence to suit the needs of her family and to highlight her collection of antique furniture. In the long, narrow house there is a pleasant series of moods. Formal yet intimate rooms coexist comfortably with stark white spaces, and everything is unified by the natural beauty seen all year round through many walls of glass. "I wanted the outdoors to be the focal point," explains the designer. "It seemed a shame to be on this beautiful hill and not bring the mountains and the trees inside."

To achieve her vision Mrs. Mellon spent two years working with a carpenter and a contractor, adding a new wing to the forty-year-old residence and updating everything that was old. "Because this wasn't a historic house, I felt I had some freedom — I wasn't destroying a monument." The residence was extended and shaped around a cobblestone courtyard. On the opposite side the house opens out to a flagstone walk and an elegant pool area.

The house works exactly as the designer intended. For family life and for entertaining up to twelve people comfortably, the paneled and beam-ceilinged trophy room is used most often. Except for the sofas, all the seating moves on casters and is upholstered in vinyls and durable ultrasuede, suitable, as Mrs. Mellon says, "for dogs and boots and muddy shoes." A love of wood is also evident in the careful way each piece of furniture has been nourished with beeswax feeder and polished to a rich gleam. Mrs. Mellon began collecting in the early 1960s, when, she claims, "you could get many pieces that are not available anymore." While most of her furniture was acquired from New York dealers, she had more fun going to estate sales in Pittsburgh, where, she says, it was possible to find something special under a table in a dusty corner.

In the new wing a tradition of woodworking craftsmanship has clearly been maintained. The halls, rooms and arched doorways are all lavishly paneled in local cherry that was handcarved less than twenty miles away. The parquet floor, which Mrs. Mellon designed herself, combines deep cherry with white maple and walnut in a heavy-scale herringbone pattern. The three woods are repeated in a checkerboard dentil in the cornice above as "a play on woods," says the designer. This fascination with the fanciful emerges unexpectedly in many parts of the house. There is, for example, a powder room that has a library theme. The lower walls are fitted with cherry cabinets, and above them is a dazzling trompe l'oeil rendering of library shelves. The make-believe books are of hand-tooled leather, and it took one craftsman eight months to complete the room.

"One of the reasons I've always loved decorating," says Gertrude Mellon, "is that it allows me to put a little fantasy, a little whimsy into whatever I am designing. I think anything taken too seriously is boring." And indeed there is nothing boring about Woodlea, where dramatic views change with the seasons and graceful and inventive interiors offer a continual invitation to discovery. The house expresses both the authentic feeling of Pennsylvania antiquity and the elegant imagination of its owner/designer. It is personal in every sense.

In the rustic southwest corner of Pennsylvania stands Woodlea, the 100-acre Colonial-style estate and private residence of interior designer Gertrude A. Mellon. PRECEDING PAGE: *A profusion of autumn glory surrounds the hilltop home.* RIGHT: *An upper-landing window provides a view of the swimming pool and the thickly wooded hills stretching beyond.*

Cool white walls, marble flooring and light filtering through an undraped window enhance the elegantly achromatic Entrance Hall. A gilded eagle perched on the newel post of the curving staircase faces a white eagle console and a pair of handcarved chairs.

In the Living Room, an 18th-century English scrollwork coat of arms glows against the brilliantly colored wall. English antiques, including two 18th-century brass-based pedestal tables, add to the baronial splendor; cool porcelains are ranged on the elaborately carved mantel.

Recalling the type of country life that might have been lived 200 years ago, a striking 18th-century English hunting-scene screen above a lavish silk damask camel-back sofa dominates another Living Room wall. A silk Tabriz rug picks up the room's vivid colors.

LEFT: *The Dining Room's landscape wallcovering depicting a seaport brings a maritime vitality to the room. The 19th-century Federal mantelpiece was acquired from a Pittsburgh home of the early 1800s. Graceful Chippendale chairs surround the 18th-century English mahogany dining table.* ABOVE: *Placed close to the undraped windows, a Sheraton breakfast table and twin Chippendale chairs share a small portion of the dining room. From this secluded area diners can enjoy the varied beauties of the changing seasons.*

BELOW: *In the Master Bath, brightly colored walls dramatize a rare collection of 19th-century sailors' valentines made from seashells. The antique English white-gold table and chair, shaped like clamshells, extend the room's delightfully nautical theme.*

OPPOSITE: *A first-floor Guest Room is bathed in a golden autumnal radiance. Richly patterned draperies, upholstery and wallcovering are an effective contrast to the plain pale tones of the ceiling and carpeting and the smooth luster of the Queen Anne furniture.*

BELOW: Mirrors extend a trompe l'oeil library, creating a seemingly endless array of books in this imposing Powder Room. Eight months were required for one craftsman to complete the leather book spines, hand-tooled with elaborate designs and humorous titles.

RIGHT: In the upstairs Guest Room, a 19th-century canopied bed—discovered in a barn and restored to its original beauty—has a pineapple, a symbol of welcome, carved into each of its posts. A collection of American and English miniature furniture, including chests of drawers, chairs and a sofa, give a fairy-tale elegance to the room; all the full-size furniture is Early American. The painting over the mantel is an American primitive.

ONE BOLD STROKE

The special talent of every young interior designer often shows itself in the imaginative handling of small and difficult spaces. Unspoiled by limitless budgets and triplexes overlooking Central Park or Rittenhouse Square, they forge their design strategies with rigor, precision and, sometimes, brilliance. The small New York apartment of Andrew Tauber exemplifies the triumph of one such designer over what might appear to be an impossible space.

His remarkable lodging is in New York's Murray Hill, a district abounding with studios carved from the townhouses of a once grand neighborhood. Taking one of these studios, which had little more to recommend it than a working fireplace and a lack of the cornices and moldings that usually clutter such New York houses, Mr. Tauber created an intimate setting of elegance and great warmth. "In a city like New York," says the designer, "with many small apartments lacking architectural interest, the more you obliterate the background, the more you can work with it." This point of view explains the total blackout of every background element, providing a calculated point of departure as well as an unexpected potential for dramatic color accents.

For the background the designer believes in using only one color — in this case, black — which he then animates with "little shots of everything else." There are many subtle counterpoints: the blues and whites of Chinese porcelains, the pastels of a flowered screen, the muted tones of antique Oriental rugs. "Black," Mr. Tauber points out, "can often become a real color. It lets a collection stand out. I don't like strong colors happening all at once. I dislike print explosions with two hundred house plants. That's not decoration. In smaller spaces you have to be calm, unless you like to change things every year. For me, however, there must be no patterns that become boring after a week. Patterns can come from porcelains and Chinese scrolls, from a flower or simply from an unusual play of light."

Andrew Tauber freely admits that the extreme elegance of the black background of his home might not be the solution for every space. It does seem ideal for his small apartment, however, creating a quietly dramatic backdrop for a noteworthy collection. "If you have a large and classic room, it's all right to paint it pale lettuce green, but few people have that," the designer explains. "The success of this space is based on an 'educated' approach to interior design. Getting a feeling of what's appropriate is, I think, being 'educated.'"

He jokingly defines his own taste as aiming at "something between Pauline de Rothschild and Rose Cumming." He admires the former's restrained perfection, the latter's animated and harmonious mixture of period styles. Understatement does play a role in Andrew Tauber's design logic, but his sense of visual drama and placement plays an important role as well. "It's fine to put things where they shouldn't be," he says. "By placing brackets near the ceiling, for example, I've pulled the room up." Measured gestures of this kind have maximum design impact. A picture hung low on a screen panel gives a sense of place to an intimate dining area; an overscaled concrete garden column, topped by a vase holding two exceptionally long and spiky flowers, brings everything into clear focus with a sudden flare of visual bravura.

In spite of the obvious drama, in spite of the flourishes of the designer's broad vocabulary, the atmosphere of the small apartment is one of quietly persuasive charm. It is, as Andrew Tauber says, "a lovely place to come back to after the day's work, something serene, something your own."

PRECEDING PAGE: *In his one-room Manhattan apartment, designer Andrew Tauber spotlights his collection of fine antiques against the effective contrast of a dramatic black matte background.*

RIGHT: *An 18th-century Chinese lacquer table provides a base for a precise arrangement that includes three K'ang Hsi celadon bottles detailed with peach-bloom dragons. A Ming painting of a sage and his attendants heating wine captures the tones of the 19th-century Cabistan rug.*

OPPOSITE: *The handpainted foliage and wildlife of an 18th-century three-panel chinoiserie screen brighten the intimate Dining Area. The setting of Ch'ien Lung porcelains graces a table draped with black moiré.*

ON A GREEK ISLAND

On the Greek island of Patmos there is a saying: "With one stone you make a sill, with two a bridge, with three a staircase; with four stones, and a big cross above, a monumental entrance to your home." In other words, take what you need — no more. Take it locally and use it without artifice.

Interior designer John Stefanidis, in heeding this tradition, has become something of a leader in the resurgence of local pride in the indigenous architecture of Patmos. For his own house, and for all the houses he restores and builds on this remote island, he puts aside sophisticated European ideas in favor of the local methods used for centuries in Patmos. The present house, his most recent restoration for a client, is beautifully situated on the edge of a hillside town clustering around the monastery of St. John the Divine. Originally it consisted of two houses, one above the other, which differ by centuries — in years and in style. The lower house was built in the seventeenth century; at that time seafaring men often built substantial houses, but had little or no inclination to embellish them. Doors and windows are becomingly rough and plain. The upper house, on the other hand, was built in the nineteenth century. By that time the trading ships had brought in a great deal from Europe, and merchants wanted the latest refinements from London and Paris. Windows and doors have all the architectural niceties of moldings, panels and cornices. To European eyes these details are just sufficiently rough-hewn to harmonize comfortably with the traditional.

The forms of the lower house are those that have been on Patmos for generations. A long curving shelf in a former storeroom, for example, has become a base for cushions in the new sitting room. The whitewash always drips onto the floor, and Mr. Stefanidis has swept it along in the traditional way.

"I always do this, even in new houses," he says. "The white becomes like a skirting. The best type of vernacular architecture has a molded effect anyway." Patmos itself is the source for everything the designer has used: simple wooden chairs, cotton fabrics, occasionally a treasured example of some fine old craft. The great days of sea trading brought rugs and furniture, paintings and sculpture from Italy, Asia Minor and Russia. "The wrought-iron beds and the Venetian chair were all imports from Italy, but I found them here," says John Stefanidis. "I feel my main contribution is to have encouraged a revival of the local techniques that have died out over the last century. Really, it's a question of making the workmen build in the way they always have. Take the handmade brick floor tiles: They have wonderfully irregular patterns, either stamped into them or made by running fingers across them before they are finally set."

There are other traditional arts — embroidery, wood carving, painting — that will always be part of the past. Even in Patmos people simply do not have time for such work now, and it may be that they no longer have the interest. The old Patmian embroideries were large hangings and bedcovers, work that today would be economically unfeasible. How does Mr. Stefanidis feel about this? "It is a loss, of course," he says thoughtfully. "It is remarkable that there is any place at all where people still make things by hand. But I do have a carpenter here on Patmos. I say that I want a bed and I give him a sketch and measurements — that is enough."

Thus, even in these changing times, the island of Patmos maintains a special degree of independence and pride of craftsmanship. For this reason the area will always be a little remote — and faithful to its own unique and time-honored traditions.

PRECEDING PAGE: *A sunlit hilltop monastery commands a splendid view from above the village of Chora on the Aegean island of Patmos. Here, using local craftsmen, designer John Stefanidis has created a house from two buildings whose history spans three centuries.*

ABOVE LEFT AND RIGHT: *Views of the Garden Courtyard illustrate the varied uses of local stone and the abundance of vegetation. Light washes the house, which is a coupling of a stark 17th-century lower structure and a 19th-century European-influenced upper half.*

ABOVE: *An exterior stairway was enclosed to form the Staircase Hall linking the 17th- and 19th-century segments of the house.* ABOVE RIGHT: *Once a storeroom, the Sitting Room contains a platform that now functions as a banquette. The whitewashed "skirting" around the floor was executed in the island's traditional style.*

OPPOSITE ABOVE: *In another view of the sitting room, the Bokhara hanging and Venetian chair and table, acquired on Patmos, attest to centuries of sea trade.* OPPOSITE BELOW: *The simplicity of the Kitchen gives it a modern sculptural quality. Pottery from Samos and locally made furnishings equip the rustic room.*

ABOVE AND LEFT: *A Bedroom in the upper house is done in dazzling white. The bed is a 19th-century Italian import; its crocheted cover was made on the island. Softly stippled door and window moldings are the result of Stefanidis's revival of an old village craft.* OPPOSITE ABOVE AND OPPOSITE BELOW LEFT: *Dining alfresco in the stone-paved Courtyard surrounded by fragrant citrus is one of the advantages of the casual island lifestyle. Apertures in the wall frame the Aegean view.* OPPOSITE BELOW RIGHT: *The view from the courtyard terrace evokes a sense of timelessness — of a land where one might still find fragments of an ancient civilization.*

A DIPLOMAT'S HOME

The late David Bruce, one of the most outstanding United States diplomats of this century, was a dedicated and versatile public servant. Through almost three decades—from 1948 until little more than a year before his death in December 1977—his official career encompassed an astonishing number of the highest and most difficult of government assignments. These ranged from the post of administrator of the Marshall Plan in Paris to that of United States representative to NATO in Brussels, and included ambassadorships to France, West Germany and the Court of St. James.

Cultured, blessed with assured but unassuming manners, David Bruce was a generous and charming host and a natural, unaffected connoisseur. Although he was a tireless negotiator and advocate, he would just as soon talk about furniture, books and paintings as about world trends or contemporary politics. Throughout Mr. Bruce's postwar career, Mrs. Bruce, who still lives in the Washington house that was their permanent home headquarters, accompanied her husband on his many missions. The daughter of a former United States career diplomat and an English mother whose family has been well known in the annals of the British North Country since the Norman Conquest, Evangeline Bruce had been inured since early youth to both the splendors and the trials of official life. As an ambassador's wife she played her part with ease, charm and marvelous efficiency, combining an American woman's practicality and resourcefulness with an English-woman's gift for relaxed control. Mrs. Bruce has an enviable beauty, a natural elegance and a distinctively individual style. She shared her husband's talent for making friends, unofficial as well as official, and her house in Washington today—like the embassies in the past—is run in a seemingly effort-

less manner. Her sense of the fitting and of the becoming stops short of rigid perfectionism, however; as she says, "I don't mind *mended* things."

In the Federal period the house was a modest but well-found farmhouse, and its picturesque little smokehouse still stands. The main building has been enlarged more than once—most recently in 1959 and 1960, when the Bruces added a considerable extension to the south. The expansion of the house "just happened," says Mrs. Bruce. "Nothing was planned." But on the street side none of the new work shows; there is only a homogeneous fa-çade of red brick in the best Georgetown tradition, with a white trim and a snug half-covering of ivy.

The material contents of the house include some exceptional pieces, including a pair of priceless early-Georgian commodes which are equaled only by a similar pair in the Victoria and Albert Museum. There are also innumerable mementos of three decades of diplomatic life—signed photographs of Queen Elizabeth II and the Duke of Edinburgh; of President Vincent Auriol and Chancellor Konrad Adenauer; of Presidents Eisenhower and Kennedy; and news photographs of David Bruce with Mao Tse-tung and Chou En-lai. For the rest, to anyone acquainted with some of England's most comfortable and attractive country houses the prevailing decorative idiom will be pleasantly familiar with its eighteenth-century European furniture and pictures; chinoiserie and Chippendale; chintz and cotton.

Mysteriously, the house has a way of denoting not simply a taste in furnishing, but a taste in friends. Aesthetically, it has the classical advantage of providing a wide range of personal choice within conventional and traditional limits. As it was during David Bruce's lifetime, so it is today—the center of a charmed circle, a twentieth-century oasis.

PRECEDING PAGE: *A memento-filled Hall typifies the Washington, D.C., home of the late career diplomat David Bruce and his wife, Evangeline.* RIGHT: *The Drawing Room offers several inviting conversation areas, including one centered around an 18th-century fireplace. Here, friends often gathered when the Bruces were home between diplomatic missions.*

RIGHT: *Two additional drawing room groupings share a richness of tone, though each has its individual motif of subdued hues. The elegant draperies were created especially for this room by an old and dear friend, the late designer John Fowler.*

ABOVE: *One of the Drawing Room's three Bessarabian rugs unifies this seating composition. A pair of 18th-century English Gothic chairs stands out vividly against two late-18th-century chinoiserie screens, used here in the European manner to fend off drafts from open doorways.*

ABOVE: *Cherished mementos of Mr. Bruce's long diplomatic service include a signed photograph of Queen Elizabeth II and photos of Mr. Bruce with Winston Churchill, Mao Tse-tung and other heads of state.*

LEFT: *In a small Sitting Room, an Early Georgian commode displays not only photos of Presidents Kennedy and Eisenhower and Secretary of State Dean Acheson, but also a Chinese "No Smoking" sign from Peking.* ABOVE: *A bow and ribbon suspending a French clock add an amusing touch to Mrs. Bruce's Bedroom.*

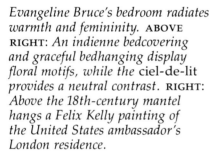

Evangeline Bruce's bedroom radiates warmth and femininity. ABOVE RIGHT: *An indienne bedcovering and graceful bedhanging display floral motifs, while the* ciel-de-lit *provides a neutral contrast.* RIGHT: *Above the 18th-century mantel hangs a Felix Kelly painting of the United States ambassador's London residence.*

RESTORATION IN TORONTO

Yorkville, in midtown Toronto, is perhaps the most dramatic example of the city's current love affair with its past. And interior designer Robert Dirstein's home on Hazelton Avenue — one of the city's most fashionable addresses — is an impressive reincarnation of that past. Incorporated in 1853, Yorkville was originally a small village on the outskirts of Toronto, its houses a typical Ontario village mix of stuccoed cottages, modest two-story structures and a few grander brick dwellings of the local gentry. After amalgamating with Toronto in 1883, Yorkville was rapidly swallowed up. When most of the wealthier residents moved to other neighborhoods and their former homes became rooming houses, the former village sank into seediness. All this was changed in the early 1970s, however, when Yorkville's old houses were converted into boutiques, restaurants and art galleries, usually with apartments on the upper floors. The streets are now thronged.

To Robert Dirstein, time is a continuum. Having known many old houses, and having been familiar with his old brownstone long before it became his, he is unintimidated by their antiquity. If the architecture of his house expresses the tastes and outlook of the gentleman who built it around 1884, Mr. Dirstein chose it because he and that original owner shared common ideals: permanence and classicism. "The house was practically disintegrating when I bought it," says the designer. "Plaster falling off the walls, doors everywhere, dark and dingy. But Hazelton is a beautiful street — it has so many trees — and I've always loved this neighborhood. And I liked the space, the extravagance of it. Look at the ceilings; they're almost eleven feet high."

The apartment's overall impression of space and comfortable elegance is effected more by optical illusion than by physical means. The interior design is the joint work of Mr. Dirstein and James Robertson, who joined the firm of Robert Dirstein & Partners about five years ago. "The living room was basically a very tall, narrow room," says Mr. Dirstein. "We have widened it by replacing a heavy old fireplace with a little white French fireplace and by choosing furniture that is light in scale." Light colors and reflective surfaces also help to maintain a sense of freedom and airiness. The entrance hall, as a matter of fact, is flooded with light: Not only is the ceiling mirrored, but there are mirror panels in the French doors. Reflections play upon reflections, transforming a dark Victorian hall into a space filled with life.

Not everything has been transformed, however. "I do prefer antiques," the designer says. "They represent the craftsmanship of the past, and you get a quality you don't find in furniture turned out in present-day factories." Love of antiquity and respect for the craftsmanship of the past aside, there is evidence that Robert Dirstein has not been entirely overawed by the artistic offerings of the rest of the world. Among the many beautiful and rare things he owns are some whose appeal is partly humorous: the Worcestershire plate whose gilt border frames a picture of a puppy; the plastic sphinx on the second floor landing; the butcher's table that still displays the marks of the carving knife on its marble top.

"I like houses to have a feeling that they belong to someone," says Robert Dirstein. Secure in his loyalty to his chosen part of the city, he has garnered the best elements from each era of Yorkville's history and blended them into a home that combines the graciousness of the past with the vitality of the present. Quiet colors, wide perspectives and the light touch of humor convey the sense of a man at home in his own and other eras. Indeed, this house on Hazelton Avenue is "a house that belongs to someone."

When Canadian designer Robert Dirstein renovated his 1884 brownstone home in Toronto's Yorkville Village, he employed optical illusions to maximize limited space. **PRECEDING PAGE:** *Mirrors on walls and ceiling are effective devices for expanding the Entrance Hall.*

OPPOSITE: *A large bay window extends the Living Room. Light-colored ceiling and dado and sunny vinyl wallcovering create a fresh background for traditional furnishings.* BELOW: *An 18th-century Italian mirror reflects the refined appointments of the Dining Room.*

The Library's dark lacquered walls showcase a collection of early-19th-century botanical creamware plates and sauceboats, and vivid fabrics flood the room with color. A marble French Directoire mantelpiece is a delicate focal point.

OPPOSITE: *Encompassing the house's entire third floor, the spacious Master Bedroom is bathed in daylight that pours in through skylights over the bed. The glowing wood floors, muted fabrics and sloped ceilings achieve a sense of intimacy, despite the room's generous proportions.*

MADAME CASTAING CHEZ ELLE

In the international world of the *antiquaire* and the interior designer there are few men and women who have achieved a legendary status, a status based not on talent alone but on a flair that almost defies definition. One of this elite is surely Mme. Madeleine Castaing of Paris, although she herself would no doubt be the first to deny it.

Her house forms the northeast angle of the rue Bonaparte and the rue Jacob, and the ground floor lies slightly below street level. As is true of many similar corners on the Left Bank in Paris, the place is, in part, an antiques shop. But the view through the windows has such an intriguingly intimate quality that one almost hesitates to push open the street door for fear of disturbing a party of amiable ghosts or interrupting the plot of a long-forgotten novel. And perhaps this odd presentiment is not all that absurd, for the talent of Madeleine Castaing is indeed an exceptionally private and personal one. The world that her imagination has created, both for herself and for her clients, has an undeniable affinity with the leisurely background of nineteenth-century European country-house fiction.

The furniture in the ground-floor shop is arranged in a series of seemingly lived-in rooms. On the second floor, however, an enfilade of high-ceilinged tall-windowed reception rooms is furnished as an apartment. But Mme. Castaing herself actually lives in a suite on the entresol between the shop and the second floor, from which she emerges in the afternoons to work and receive visitors. Her clients are an infinitely varied human collection but, in her words, "they have one thing in common — sensibility — and they tend to be very faithful." Past clients have included Jean Cocteau, for whom she decorated a house at Milly, and Mme. Francine Weisweiller, for whom she worked at Saint-Jean-Cap-Ferrat and in Paris. More recently she has worked on townhouses, apartments and small houses in Belgium and Switzerland as well as in France.

Her remarks about her general technique as a decorator are spontaneous and direct: "I have to know the people, and I have to like them. I look at the house or the apartment and the surroundings — and wait for inspiration. If the people are worth the trouble, inspiration invariably comes. I have picked up quite a little psychological sense in the course of the last thirty-five years. I don't like to work for people who simply want an interior that will improve their standing in the eyes of others.

"I don't think there are any rules in design except that the desire to surprise or shock takes a decorator nowhere at all," Mme. Castaing says. "Personally, I just follow my instinct, amuse myself creating an atmosphere, mix up all sorts of things I like. It is important to be inspired by *things*. Obviously, a good decorator needs sound professional knowledge, and I myself have a great respect for the profession. But for me the real point of departure is poetry, a stroke from some magic wand. One must let the heart have its say in all matters."

Even a total stranger, watching Madeleine Castaing as she moves about the apartment, finds it impossible not to fall under her spell. Perhaps because these rooms serve her principally as a private theater or experimental workshop, they seem to partake of the endearingly unpremeditated quality of a charade. Instead of asserting themselves as potentially priceless works of twentieth-century art, for example, the powerful Soutine canvases on the wall assume the status of pictures in a family album. Although a doyenne of the decorating profession, Mme. Castaing can still call to mind a little girl of years ago — blissfully absorbed in "playing houses."

Mme. Castaing's Paris apartment is the consummate example of le style anglais, *the late-18th-century revival mode of design for which she is noted.* PRECEDING PAGE: *In the Gallery, tall windows covered with 19th-century French floral-painted shades are balanced by the bookshelves opposite. A skillful mixture of 19th-century antiques creates an inviting progression to the salon beyond.* RIGHT: *The gracious Salon conjures images of genteel Victorian gatherings. The precisely arranged furnishings include an 18th-century English settee, a Victorian fringed pouf and an Austrian Schönbrunn-style canapé; a Second Empire lacquer tray on a stand is used as a table for drinks. The Soutine paintings are an arresting contrast to the rest of the appointments.*

Another view of the Salon reveals a fireplace surrounded by a perfectly symmetrical arrangement of elements: A 19th-century overmantel mirror is the central focus, framed by pairs of Russian malachite candlesticks, 18th-century French vases and English Regency cabinets.

An atmosphere of mellowed richness pervades the Game Room, the ideal spot for an evening's diversion. An 18th-century porcelain stove warms the high-ceilinged room, whose distinctive décor includes Viennese mahogany chairs and a rare enamel Directoire billiard lamp.

All the paintings on Mme. Castaing's walls are the work of Chaim Soutine, a frequent houseguest who often painted in the garden and used his hostess as a model. Three examples of his work are displayed to advantage in the Dining Room.

Mme. Castaing's Bedroom, painted and draped in quiet pastels, contains furniture that once belonged to a cousin of Napoleon III. A 19th-century bronze doré chandelier, suspended over the room like a gilded blossom, draws attention to the cloudlike pattern of the ceiling.

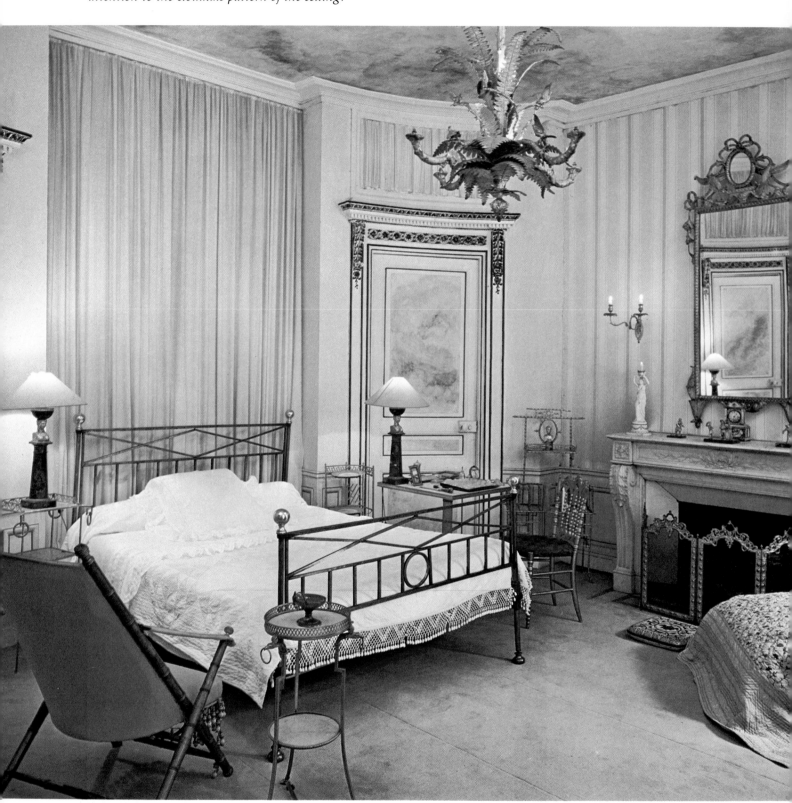

Two more paintings by Soutine, one of them reflected in the 19th-century giltwood Adam mirror, grace the Bedroom. The mantel holds antiques, including an 18th-century mother-of-pearl clock and Russian malachite candlesticks.

Handsome draperies accentuate the high vaulted ceiling in the Bath. The sconce next to the faux-bamboo-framed mirror is done in an unusual style of etching on glass called lithophanie. *The distinctive fixtures are all of gleaming bronze gilt.*

ECHOES OF BALMORAL

Some thirty miles south from Edinburgh, first city of the Scots and the presumptive capital of an independent Scotland, stands the house called *Glen*. It is the seat of the Tennant family and the distinguished yet comfortable home of the Honorable Colin Tennant, heir to the barony of Glenconner, and of his wife, Lady Anne, eldest daughter of the fifth earl of Leicester, and of their five children.

Glen is an imposing example of the style called Scottish Baronial. Its hallmarks — turrets, towers and forbidding high stone walls — are generally associated with Balmoral, the royal residence on the Deeside. Balmoral was certainly not without its admirers. Indeed, one of the most common sights etched against Scotland's windy skies is the decorative fortifications of wealthy Victorian landowners' mansions in similar nineteenth-century style. Glen, perhaps the epitome of this style, was begun in 1851 to the designs of David Bryce, and in fact predates Balmoral by several years. Now, some hundred years later, Glen is still impressive, but the livery and the pomp have gone. It is a family home today. The children play in the reception rooms, and Lady Anne darns their socks in the drawing room.

Thus the story of Glen is a story of transformation. Perhaps the most important event in this transformation was the coming, in the 1930s, of Mr. Tennant's stepmother, Elizabeth Glenconner. The lady herself had many fresh ideas, and she had as mentor Syrie Maugham, wife of Somerset, a woman whose influence on interior design was so prodigious that its effect is still being felt today, and not only in the United Kingdom. Anything dark, drab or heavy was anathema to her: Out went the extensive paneling that cloaked the hall at Glen, and in its place came cool paint and pots of pale flowers. Lady Glenconner wanted simplicity, so in the drawing room there are no ceiling cornices and, instead of traditional bookcases enriched with leather tooling and surmounted by goblets and paintings, there are elegant shelves flush with the walls. Only the library entirely escaped the innovations; here, one suspects, his lordship's will prevailed. A heavy desk fitted with Victorian accessories, stout wooden bookcases and paintings no one was expected to look at remain exactly as they were before Syrie Maugham and her disciples had ever been heard of. Unchanged, too, is the magnificent William Morris carpet, which is one of the superb glories of Glen.

Also from the nineteenth century are the labeled bells, more than forty of them, that line the tiled kitchen hall. But none rings today. The house that to Lord Rosebery of Mentmore was "the most comfortable I have ever stayed in" now manages almost without servants. The changes begun by his stepmother continue under Mr. Tennant. The tower has been shut, and Mr. Tennant would like to pull it down. In storms, the wind tugs at the battlements and roars in the flues, and there is nothing that can be done about that. There is generous central heating, but the area of cultivated garden has been cut to a minimum. Although a great collector — he acquired the fine Landseer that hangs in the hall and the Wemyss pottery to be found in every bedroom — Mr. Tennant's aim is to simplify. It is his desire to keep up with the times. Queen Victoria has been dead a long time, and surely Great Britain is not what it once was. And so it is with Glen.

But still, much of the noble splendor of old remains: Some nine thousand acres guard the Tennants' privacy; high grouse moors enclose their home and deer stalk the hills. The past is far from gone, but at Glen it has been put to the most graceful and pleasing of contemporary uses.

PRECEDING PAGE: *Glen, the home of the Honorable Colin Tennant and his family, was designed in 1851 by architect David Bryce. The 35-room baronial residence exemplifies the mid-19th-century Scottish preference for decorative fortifications embellished with turrets and towers.*

BELOW: *Although arches and columns lend an aura of grandeur to the Entrance Hall, the dominant tone is relatively informal. Sparing appointments—a French cabinet and a chest of drawers, both 18th century—contribute to the sense of comfort and simplicity.*

BELOW: *In the Dining Room, paintings by Allan Ramsay, Richard Wilson and Sir David Wilkie reinforce the 19th-century aesthetic of Victorian Gothic Revival chairs and a William and Adelaide period table.* BOTTOM: *Edwardian bells recall the days of large domestic staffs.*

OPPOSITE: *The only room that has not been modernized, the Library retains its original bookcases and a William Morris rug woven for Mr. Tennant's great-grandparents. A Regency Gothic writing table and moody chiaroscuro portraits extend the retrospective atmosphere.*

RIGHT: *A pelican finial perches on the centerpost of a spiral staircase that was added to the residence in 1906. Nearby, tiers of 18th-century mezzotints by George Morland enhance a vivid background with graphic intensity.*

RIGHT: *In the Valley Bedroom, a family double portrait carved in marble hangs above the mantel. The many compartments of a writing table/bookcase contain fine examples of an extensive Wemyssware collection. A draped and canopied 18th-century four-poster frames the composition.*

Topiary, balustrades, rose bushes and colorful potted plants accent the south lawn of the Garden, which recedes into a lush, hilly landscape. As the Tennant family estate comprises a total of 9,000 acres, Glen is ringed in privacy and buffered by natural beauty.

DECOR FOR MANHATTAN

Interior designer David Whitcomb's point of view, particularly about his own Beekman Place duplex in Manhattan—four large rooms plus a dramatic entrance hall—has gone through several changes. "I even moved out once, I got so bored with it—but then I moved back," he says. "I don't know that I have a particular word for my style. I certainly don't like the word *eclectic,* so let's simply say that what I have here is a collection of dissimilar pieces, both as to country of origin and period of time. I'm very particular about what I want around me, even to the simplest things. I feel that everything in a room should have some meaning for the owner—objects one loves, not just things that have been acquired because they are rare or expensive."

David Whitcomb is speaking in his upstairs living room, a lovely area fitted with double-glazed walls, a vast fireplace banked with hidden stereo speakers, a whimsical Zuber wallpaper screen, a massive English table, a sofa of Mexican cotton that doubles as a bed, and sang de boeuf vases towering on pedestals. Perhaps most striking is the monastic quality of the room. The scale is silently grand, imposing and seductive, but the designer has clarified and purified the living room with heavy editing. A new painting, proudly hung over the English table, prompted Mr. Whitcomb to remove a brightly colored curtain and take away a large rug. "I decided to shrink the room, to make it less formal, more intimate. I took the rug away and left the random-width oak floor bare, 'covering' it with the coffee table." He points to a large fabric-covered and lacquered table that he has adapted from a book on Chinese furniture.

"You see," the designer says, "a pretty room is not enough any more—it also has to be useful. Today people want comfort without a great deal of maintenance. I look at a room as a container. Now, this particular room may look 'pretty,' but it is actually very useful. For example, take the table. Guests can sit on it or put their feet up on it—and I use it for all my books. And they're *not* just decorative," he says emphatically; "I actually read them! Although I don't have a lot of it here, I do love furniture, and enjoy buying it for other people."

Down the hall from the living room is the designer's library/bedroom, a mixture of many delightful details—paintings, porcelains and sculptures of dogs. It is a room where Mr. Whitcomb reads biographies or books on politics and where guests come after dinner to have a drink or play Chi Chi, a Chinese fortune-telling game. The atmosphere here is quiet, cheerful and, like all the other rooms, welcoming. Mr. Whitcomb works out of his house, where projects for private apartments and homes are frequently spread out on the circular dining table downstairs, its top a handpainted mural of birds in a leafy tree. "There is something very American about working at this table. Somehow it seems like the old days, like a table where the father read the newspaper, the children did their homework, and the whole family ate together. That feeling really appeals to me. My table is as often covered with samples and plans as it is with china and glass."

David Whitcomb freely admits that privacy is an essential element in his own life, which surely explains the serene, cocoonlike environment he has created for himself. "I enjoy my work tremendously, and I'm happy my life isn't filled with all those two-hour three-martini luncheons. The process of design is naturally a creative one, so I suppose it makes for a certain amount of ego. Although I'm proud of what I do, I don't think that needs to be interpreted as egotism. I do feel that clients come to me partly because they *already* have taste."

Beauty, comfort and practicality coexist in designer David Whitcomb's low-keyed and elegant Manhattan townhouse on Beekman Place. PRECEDING PAGE: *A folding screen covered with wallpaper inspires flights of tropical fantasy in the subtle-hued Living Room.*

LEFT: *Draperies and a garden view form a varied background in the living room for an 18th-century painting by Johann Falch, an antique English console and the graceful silhouette of a classical urn perched on a tall pedestal.* BELOW LEFT: *Another living room wall offers aesthetic polarities: a nonobjective painting by Claudio Bravo and an 18th-century English portrait of four musicians. The design of the central table was inspired by Chinese domestic furniture.*

OPPOSITE: *Several Dining Room views reveal the attention lavished on architectural detailing: Rough-hewn wood and brick lend warmth to walls; travertine gives floors a cool sleekness; and mirrored pilasters serve both to unify the space and punctuate the long wall of window facing the garden. An unusual dining table dominates: Its base is a machinery model found by chance in the countryside. Regency chairs surround it, imparting a classical grace to the sparely appointed room. An extensive collection of mercury glass and a Martin Carey drawing fill one corner with concentrated detail.*

*Spotlighting, deep shadows and the architectonic form
of a steel-balustraded stairway enhance the drama of
a still-life arrangement poised on a platform in the
Entrance Hall. The French glazed-ceramic caryatids and
a mirror-faceted sphere recall 19th-century Romanticism.*

A BARONESS'S LONDON FLAT

A few private and very quiet rooms; a secluded, even secret, place to withdraw from a busy life. We all dream of it, but Rothschild dreams have a way of becoming reality. Not long before she died, Pauline de Rothschild created such a refuge of exquisite beauty for herself. In a flat in Albany, the exclusive London residential landmark, her genius for bringing beauty to everything around her blossomed once again, this time in quiet privacy.

Her husband, Baron Philippe de Rothschild, explains: "Her life was always so busy. In Paris and at Mouton, the château near Bordeaux, there were always many people—our friends, all the wine enthusiasts. She loved London and came here to rest. This flat was kept for herself, for her own personal satisfaction. It should be recorded. For this flat is the distillation, the 'point' of all the work and thought of her entire life—her house in New York, her ten years with Hattie Carnegie, her apartment in Paris, the new rooms we did together at Mouton."

There is one essential difference in these London rooms. Her other houses are gregarious; this is introspective. Mouton is always ready to receive dozens of guests. Pauline de Rothschild entertained at tables of unique charm, choosing from one hundred and seventy services of china and the finest linens. A full-time flower arranger carried out her instructions to produce the famous "landscape tables," with centerpieces of moss and country heather. Dozens of little flowers in Japanese enamel vases might be lined up along the length of the table, or an arrangement of vegetables—curly lettuce or cabbage— might replace flowers to give a fresh, vivid green.

The London flat is very different. There is but one set of simple blue-and-white china, and only a bowl of fruit as a centerpiece. This theme of simplicity is seen throughout the flat. One spray of lilies in a jug or a handful of freesias in a lined wicker basket is enough. There are only two paintings, and one is very small; the baroness felt there was too much art in evidence in Paris and at Mouton. "The one significant painting that is here," says Baron de Rothschild, "I bought for her. It is very large, and I thought it would look wonderful over the sofa. Anyone else might have put it there, but not Pauline. She hung it in her own bedroom, the smallest room in the flat, where it extends from floor to ceiling."

The rooms are off the "Ropewalk" at the back of Albany and were designed by Henry Holland in 1802. Pauline de Rothschild was fully appreciative of the proportions, the advantages and the limitations each room offered. Because the corridor is narrow, her husband's bedroom, just to the right of the front entrance, was made very elegant so that the door could be left open as often as possible, thus extending the space. She used her own bedroom at the end of this corridor to draw the eye forward, always leaving the door open and a lamp lit beyond it.

It was not a small effort, bringing such unique color and style to these rooms, and the late decorator John Fowler was of inestimable value to the baroness. Together they discussed everything, letting ideas evolve slowly; both were perfectionists. "She wouldn't have achieved anything of this kind without John Fowler and all his craftsmen," says Philippe de Rothschild. "If you had asked her, she would have said it was all to his credit. I suspect John Fowler would have said it was *her* genius. I would say it is the result of a remarkable cooperation."

Beauty, elegance and the pleasures of the eye were always at the heart of the life Pauline and Philippe de Rothschild shared. It is inevitable, of course, that these qualities are evident in her London flat—evident, but magnificently simplified.

The late Pauline de Rothschild's London refuge, which she created in collaboration with the renowned designer John Fowler, is described by her husband as "the distillation of all the work and thought of her life." PRECEDING PAGE AND RIGHT: *The Drawing Room, expressing the owner's personal tranquillity through its subtle tones and fabrics, is restfully uncluttered. An unconventional steel-framed, silk-upholstered sofa designed by the baroness accentuates both comfort and beauty.*

Though she entertained lavishly on the Continent,
Pauline de Rothschild reveled in her quieter London life.
Here, the baroness kept the table settings very simple.
Undraped windows in the Dining Room frame a view of a
neighboring building's classical façade, which she loved.

The baroness chose this room as her own Bedroom because, like the dining room, it faces the Corinthian-pillared residence across the way. It is also the smallest room in the flat, and its intimate proportions and neutral color scheme made it a perfect haven from the demands of a very active life.

Baron Philippe de Rothschild presented his wife with the 1741 portrait of Lady Elizabeth Montagu, by an unknown artist, that occupies a floor-to-ceiling place of honor in her bedroom. He expected her to place it in the drawing room; instead, she chose this more unconventional setting.

Because of limited space and a narrow hallway, the baron's Bedroom door is often left open to extend the flat; the room was designed with great discrimination to blend well with the rest of the décor. LEFT: An early-19th-century Japanese painting on glass is the room's only wall ornament. OPPOSITE: The walls and ceiling are painted in subdued monochromatic tones. Light bathes the silk-draped bed where the baron still likes to work on his French translations of Elizabethan poetry and modern English plays.

IN THE GRAND MANNER

It was a big, plain house on Shinnecock Bay that did not honestly merit a more evocative description than "urban brick," with a collection of oversized and overstuffed furniture that the owners' first impulse was to eliminate. Nor did the house seem entirely promising to New York interior designer George Clarkson when he was called upon to help the renowned mountaineer and explorer Dr. Walter Abbott Wood and his wife move from their home in Virginia to this new Southampton residence.

The Shinnecock Bay house had problems, and they were big problems scaled to a big house. But neither the Woods nor Mr. Clarkson lacked courage or the spirit of adventure. As a designer George Clarkson is no newcomer to challenging situations, and he brings a clear-headed sense of style to everything he does. "It was, we all knew," he recalls, "a problem house. That it was new yet not contemporary was difficult to begin with. But the house had size, with high ceilings and everything on the grand scale. The arrangement, the view and the location overlooking the bay were good. But to make it interesting was the real challenge."

The "plain, urban brick look" was the first thing to vanish, under a coat of white paint. The mullioned and transomed windows were replaced with clean sweeps of plate glass. New shutters and heavy lanterns rearticulated and lightened the façades. Doors were redesigned, and new approaches to the swimming pool and the terrace were added.

The interior of the house is based on color, and some of the designer's colors are openly assertive: the sunny tone animating the living room, the dining room's deep rosy walls and ceiling. Massed together, these strongly unifying colors would have been impossible. But the designer separated them by keeping the progression of entrance hall, gallery and enclosed terrace that opens through the center of the house a monotone of beige, greige and white. The large-patterned wallpapers were printed to blend with the sisal pattern on the terrace furniture, and the floors were repaved in white-glazed brick and white marble to continue the flow of white-lacquered woodwork. In this way, Mr. Clarkson was able to avoid strong visual confrontations.

"The Woods had beautiful furniture," he explains. "The problem with it was mostly one of arranging and bringing things up to date. It seemed that the pieces I wanted to use — the overscaled furniture from Dr. Wood's office and an old opium bed his parents had brought back from China — they really didn't want anymore." But George Clarkson has learned that in the excitement of acquiring a new house people usually give away the wrong things.

In the Woods' Southampton house, the furnishings they once wanted to discard are now the very things the interiors are built around. To Mr. Clarkson, who has a passion for anything painted white, the opium bed, cut down and lacquered, seemed an ideal start for the house. It focuses the enclosed terrace and gives a relaxed elegance to the room's white-lacquered rattan chairs and tables and the Chinese wallpaper. In the living room, oversized office sofas and chairs from the Virginia house have been re-covered in a bold chintz. An expansive white rug and the warm light of the living room give the space an air of exuberant abundance.

The house has been given a warmth and dignified elegance for its owners that updates it yet maintains a tone with which they are familiar and comfortable. George Clarkson has given the Woods what they wanted, a welcoming and animated house, at once festive and tranquil — a place for celebrations and a place for celebrating the pleasures of daily life.

Designer George Clarkson brought a spark of new life to Dr. and Mrs. Walter Abbott Wood's Southampton home. PRECEDING PAGE: *In the Entrance Hall, guarded by Chinese temple dogs, light color establishes a neutral introduction to the residence's bright palette.*

ABOVE: *A coat of white paint and new shutters refreshed the home's brick exterior.* RIGHT: *In the Living Room, the warm, glowing color of the lacquered walls and ceiling and of the silk draperies creates a unified background for commodious sofas and chairs upholstered in cheerful floral chintz. Two low tables—one rectilinear and light-hued, the other curvilinear and dark— represent interesting extremes, and each is accompanied by a nearby chair of a contrasting tone. Wooden appointments, such as the tables near the mantel, provide evenly distributed accents throughout the room.*

OPPOSITE: *Squares and circles are subtle counterpoints in the Dining Room, where the rug is a geometric network underscoring rounded motifs: the design on paneled doors of the Louis XV fruitwood armoire; the forms of the Meissen, Chinese Export and Picasso plates within; and the oval-backed Victorian chairs that surround the oval Directoire dining table. A landscape by Nessi is a departure in form and color.* LEFT: *Picasso plates celebrating the bullfight are arranged above the George II sideboard.* ABOVE: *A serene view of Shinnecock Bay is a delightful feature of the Conservatory.*

Gleaming with vivid color, Dr. Wood's imposing Study houses a collection of photographs and memorabilia that recalls his 40-year career as a mountaineer and explorer. An extensive library and a large portrait of his grandfather add to the room's serious air.

LEFT: *Delicate pastel shades brighten the warp-print fabric used in the Master Bedroom for baldachin and draperies, bedcovering and chair upholstery. In harmony with Mr. Clarkson's design philosophy, the small 18th-century French desk is both decorative and functional.* ABOVE: *Mirrors create kaleidoscopic images in Mrs. Wood's Dressing Room.*

VILLA NEAR SAINT-CLOUD

In the past this house in France was owned by the composer Charles Gounod. Perhaps the inspiration for the many garden scenes in his operas came from the villa's charming gardens, or from the vast Parc de Saint-Cloud across the way. Both the gardens and the park have certainly been a great inspiration for the present owner, Mme. Barbara Wirth.

Saint-Cloud is a western suburb of Paris, once a favorite area for kings and princes, among them Philippe I, duc d'Orléans, brother of Louis XIV, who built an immense château in the center of the park designed by Le Nôtre. The Wirth house stands where the now-demolished stables of the château were originally located. Mme. Wirth's collaborator in the décor of the house was her cousin, Christian Badin, David Hicks's associate in France. M. Badin and Mme. Wirth have close rapport. "We do everything together," she says. "Our tastes are identical." Barbara Wirth has a clearly defined sense of taste that she describes as being more English than French. "I need air, light and gaiety."

Her living room, looking out over the garden, is a mélange of colors both daring and natural. Indeed, color seems to be everywhere, and the effect is like sitting in an indoor garden. Even the tables seem part of the outdoors. There is, for example, a wonderful low bronze table with sculptured mice, frogs and lizards crawling around its legs — the work of Diégo Giacometti. Side tables covered with leather painted to resemble *faux marbre* groan under stacks of books, many of them on gardening. The house itself is kept very cool — "For plants, coolness is indispensable," says the owner — and scattered around on the backs of chairs are huge cashmere shawls, in shades of dusty rose, soft yellow and blue, for the less warm-blooded guests. The dining room also faces the garden. It is most countrified, done totally in blue and white, and resembles nothing so much as a dining room in Provence. The wallcovering is *toile de Tanlay*, made today, as it has been for centuries, by using blue fabric and bleaching the pattern into it, rather than coloring white fabric.

"I often have dinner parties three or four times a week," says Mme. Wirth. She entertains business associates of her husband, who is a chemist, but she likes to mix artists and visitors from abroad as well. In the dining room are two collections, one of English and the other of French faïence — in blue and white, of course. "This is my treasure," she says, and picks up a Louis XIV goblet, a gift from her husband. But not all of her collections are so serious. Whimsical baskets, some in comical shapes, are strewn everywhere, plucked from every part of the world where the Wirths have traveled. On the mantel are eleven leather-lines, interconnecting baskets from Mali, that are about a century old. "I simply can't go anywhere without buying baskets. I suppose there are about eighty or ninety around," says Barbara Wirth. The upstairs hallway is lined with them; they hold everything from magazines to children's toys.

The family — she and her husband, three children and one dog — have outgrown the house, and they hope to move into larger quarters. At the moment, for example, the piano is in the master bedroom. "Well, there's nowhere else for it in the house," Mme. Wirth shrugs. She adds, however, that the atmosphere of clutter is not what she and Christian Badin strive for when they work with clients. "I like softness, not glitter. And harmony. I don't like to be bowled over by any house." At present she is reconciled to giving up her garden for a Paris apartment, but the jumble of other objects will surely find a place. "I can't live without two things," claims Mme. Wirth — "geraniums and baskets!"

Located in the Parisian suburb of Saint-Cloud, the residence of interior designer Barbara Wirth epitomizes the inviting villas of France. PRECEDING PAGE: An avid gardener, Mme. Wirth accents her home's parklike grounds with pots of all-white blossoming plants.

In decorating the villa's interiors, Mme. Wirth consulted her associate and cousin, designer Christian Badin. BELOW: Plants and an abundance of books create a relaxed atmosphere that complements the Living Room's country-style décor. A durrie rug covers the stone floor.

An 18th-century Rouen jardinière and a Louis XV console give a period feeling to the Entrance Hall. The stone floor is done in the traditional manner, with black cabochon inset.

Another view of the Living Room reveals a 16th-century Italian portrait, set informally on the mantel, and a table by Giacometti, laden with books. The room is dotted with containers of scented geraniums cultivated in the greenhouse.

A crisp blue-and-white fabric drapes the round table in the Dining Room. Upholstery, draperies and wall-covering of an 18th-century pattern augment the room's pleasant provincial feeling. French doors open to a view of the sunny garden.

A sprightly floral-patterned chintz is used for bed linens,
draperies and wallcovering in the Master Bedroom.
A pair of unusual four-tiered tables topped by Giacometti
lamps flanks the bed; 17th-century Chippendale chairs
and 18th-century watercolors lend a nostalgic grace.

BELOW: *The procession of unusual baskets was collected by the Wirths during their travels.* BOTTOM: *African ivory figures and small boxes are displayed in the Master Bedroom.*

BELOW: *In the master bedroom, a cheerful fire and an American rocking chair enhance an inviting corner dominated by a Dutch ebony-framed mirror and a Louis XV mantel.*

159

CREDITS

WRITERS

The following writers prepared the original
Architectural Digest articles from which the material
in this book has been adapted:

Susan Heller Anderson
Helen Barnes
Alexander Davis
Bruno de Hamel
Elizabeth Dickson
Luis Escobar
Philippe Jullian
Rosemary Kent
Elizabeth Kimball
Elizabeth Lambert
Tina Laver
Valentine Lawford
John Loring
Suzanne Stark Morrow

All original text adapted by Sam Burchell.

Caption Writers:
Joanne Jaffe
Joyce Madison
Joyce Winkel

PHOTOGRAPHERS

Jaime Ardiles-Arce 108-113, 146-153
Jerry Bragsted 16-23
Robert Emmett Bright 10-15
Richard Champion 80-91
Bruno de Hamel 124-131
Daniel Eifert 132-137
Pascal Hinous 64-71, 72-79, 114-123, 154-159
Horst 24-35, 102-107
Russell MacMasters 50-55
Derry Moore 36-41, 56-63, 96-101, 138-145
José Luis Pérez 42-49
Irving Schild 92-95

DESIGN

Design Direction:
Philip Kaplan, Graphics Director
The Knapp Press

Book Design and Production:
Design Office/San Francisco
Bruce Kortebein
Cynthia Croker
Leigh McLellan